WHEN I DON'T DESIRE GOD

WHEN I DON'T
DESIRE GOD

How to Fight for Joy

STUDY GUIDE DEVELOPED BY DESIRING GOD

CROSSWAY BOOKS

WHEATON, ILLINOIS

When I Don't Desire God Study Guide

Copyright © 2008 by Desiring God Foundation

Published by Crossway Books
            a publishing ministry of Good News Publishers
            1300 Crescent Street
            Wheaton, Illinois 60187

This study guide is based on and is a companion to *When I Don't Desire God* by John Piper (Crossway Books, 2004).

Cover design: Amy Bristow

Cover photo: Josh Dennis

First printing, 2008

Printed in the United States of America

Scripture quotations are taken from *The Holy Bible: English Standard Version®*. Copyright © 2001 by Crossway Bibles, a publishing ministry of Good News Publishers. Used by permission. All rights reserved.

All emphases in Scripture quotations have been added by the author.

ISBN 978-1-4335-0253-8

BP		16	15	14	13	12	11	10	09	08
14	13	12	11	10	9	8	7	6	5	4	3	2	1

CONTENTS

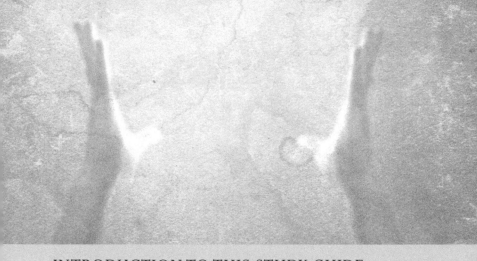

INTRODUCTION TO THIS STUDY GUIDE

MOST CHRISTIANS ARE familiar with the Greatest Commandment: "You shall love the Lord your God with all your heart and with all your soul and with all your mind" (Matthew 22:37). Some insist that this command does not mean we are obligated to enjoy God above all things. "This is a command," they say. "Joy and delight are emotions, and everyone knows that we can't command our emotions. Therefore, love must simply be a matter of deciding and not a matter of feeling."

But the Bible will not support such logic. Emotions are commanded everywhere. "*Rejoice* in the Lord always" (Philippians 4:4). "*Long* for the pure spiritual milk" (1 Peter 2:2). "*Giving thanks* always" (Ephesians 5:20). These commands, and hundreds like them, are not simply commands to *think* a certain way; they are commands to *feel* a certain way. So also, the command to love God above all else is not merely about our actions but about our hearts.

But the fact remains: we do not have ultimate control over our emotions. No matter how hard we try, our hearts are not like water faucets. We cannot simply turn them on and off at will. Nevertheless, our obligation remains. And the stakes are infinitely high. "If anyone has no love for the Lord, let him be accursed" (1 Corinthians 16:22). Eternity hangs on the presence of proper affections for God. Jesus told us that we must be born again (John 3:7). The evidence that we have been born again is that we are now able to see and savor the glory of God. Therefore, the fight for joy is not optional. It is essential.

The aim of this study guide is to aid you in your fight. The central question that we will seek to answer is this: How do you get a desire that you don't have and you can't create? How do you fight for a gift? What strategies are available to me when I don't desire God? Our prayer is that this study guide and DVD would be used by God to give profound and practical encouragement to thousands who are struggling to delight in Christ and long to be satisfied in God above all things.

This study guide is designed to be used in an eight-session,[1] guided group study that focuses on the *When I Don't Desire God* DVD set.[2] After an introductory lesson, each subsequent lesson examines one thirty-minute session[3] from the *When I Don't Desire God* DVD set.[4] You, the learner, are encouraged to prepare for the viewing of each session by reading and reflecting upon Scripture, by considering key quotations, and by asking yourself penetrating questions. Your preparatory work for each lesson is marked with the heading "Before You Watch the DVD, Study and Prepare" in Lessons 2-7.

The workload is conveniently divided into five daily (and manageable) assignments. There is also a section suggesting further study. This work is to be completed individually before the group convenes to view the DVD and discuss the material.

Throughout this study guide, paragraphs printed in a shaded box (like this one) are excerpts from a book written by John Piper or excerpts taken from the Desiring God web site. They are included to supplement the study questions and to summarize key or provocative points.

The next section in Lessons 2-7, entitled "While You Watch the DVD, Take Notes," is to be completed as the DVD is playing. This section includes fill-in-the-blanks and leaves space for note-taking. You are encouraged to engage with the DVD by filling in the appropriate blanks and writing down other notes that will aid you in the group discussion.

The third section in each normal lesson is "After You Watch the DVD, Discuss What You've Learned." Three discussion questions are provided to guide and focus the conversation. You may record, in the spaces provided, notes that will help you contribute to the conversation. Or you may use this space to record things from the discussion that you want to remember.

The final section is an application section: "After You Discuss, Make Application." You will be challenged to record a take-away point and to engage in a certain activity that is a fitting response to the content presented in the lesson.

Group leaders will want to find the Leader's Guide, included at the end of this study guide, immediately.

Life transformation will only occur by the grace of God. Therefore, we highly encourage you to seek the Lord in prayer throughout the learning process. Pray that God would open your eyes to see wonderful things in his Word. Pray that he would grant you the insight and concentration you need in order to get the most from this resource. Pray that God would cause you not to merely understand the truth but also to rejoice in it. And pray that the discussion in your group would be mutually encouraging and edifying. We've included objectives at the beginning of each lesson. These objectives won't be realized without the gracious work of God through prayer.

NOTES

1. While this study guide is ideally suited for an eight-session study, it is possible to complete it in six sessions. The Leader's Guide at the end of this study guide contains a note on one way to do this. The six-session option may be well suited for groups that are already familiar with each other or that only have six weeks to complete the study.

2. Although this resource is designed to be used in a group setting, it can also be used by the independent learner. Such learners would have to decide for themselves how to use this resource in the most beneficial way. We would suggest doing everything but the group discussion, if possible.

3. Thirty minutes is only an approximation. Some sessions are longer; others are shorter.

4. In addition to the DVD set, John Piper has also written a book entitled *When I Don't Desire God: How to Fight for Joy* (Wheaton, IL: Crossway Books, 2004). Many of the excerpts in this study guide are drawn from this book. If, after completing this study, you desire to further explore the material that you've covered, we highly recommend reading *When I Don't Desire God*. This book is available for free online at www.desiringGod.org in the Online Books section of the Resource Library.

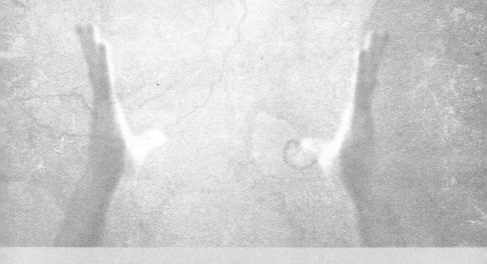

LESSON 1
INTRODUCTION TO *WHEN I DON'T DESIRE GOD*

LESSON OBJECTIVES

It is our prayer that after you have finished this lesson . . .

> › You will discover how you and others in your group view the role of joy in the Christian life.

> › Your curiosity would be roused, and questions would begin to come to mind.

> › You will be eager to learn more about how you can fight for joy in God.

ABOUT YOURSELF

1) What is your name?

2) Tell the group something about yourself that they probably don't already know.

3) Describe your relationship with Jesus.

A PREVIEW OF *WHEN I DON'T DESIRE GOD*

1) In your mind, is the fight for joy essential to the Christian life? What strategies do you use in your fight for joy?

2) In the space below, describe the current state of your relationship with Christ. What are the most significant obstacles to deeper fellowship with God? How are you seeking to overcome these obstacles? Be specific.

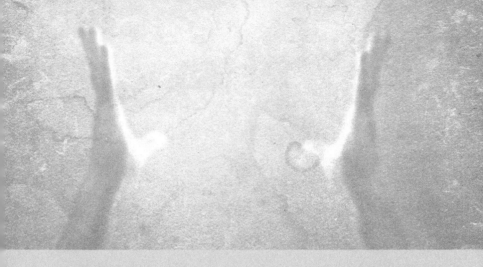

LESSON 2

THE FIGHT FOR JOY IS ESSENTIAL (PART 1)
A Companion Study to the When I Don't Desire God DVD, Session 1

LESSON OBJECTIVES

It is our prayer that after you have finished this lesson . . .

> You will embrace the truth that God seeks to display his glory in everything he does.

> You will recognize the spiritual bankruptcy of alternative approaches to the Christian life.

> You will understand more fully the nature of God's love for human beings.

BEFORE YOU WATCH THE DVD, STUDY AND PREPARE

DAY 1: HEAD AND HEART

Many Christians throughout history have struggled to bring their emotions and affections in line with their knowledge and beliefs. In his autobiography *Confessions*, Augustine put the matter like this:

I was astonished that although I now loved you . . . I did not persist in enjoyment of my God. Your beauty drew me to you, but soon I was dragged away from you by my own weight and in dismay I plunged again into the things of this world . . . as though I had sensed the fragrance of the fare but was not yet able to eat it.[1]

QUESTION 1: Have you ever felt this disconnect between your beliefs and your affections? How crucial is it that we not only know truth with our minds but also delight in truth with our hearts? Why?

"Fact! Faith! Feeling!" is a common Christian slogan that is meant to summarize the essence of the Christian life. At times the slogan appears as a train: "the locomotive is 'fact.' The coal car is 'faith.' The caboose is 'feeling.' The explanation reads: 'The train will run with or without the caboose. However, it would be futile to attempt to pull the train by the caboose.'"[2]

QUESTION 2: Interact with the above analogy. Is this an accurate portrayal of the Christian life? Why or why not? Cite Scripture in your answer.

DAY 2: ECHOES OF GLORY

QUESTION 3: Year after year, many people venture to the Grand Canyon, the Rocky Mountains, and similar places in order to gaze upon these natural wonders. Speculate on what draws people to go to these places.

Study the following passage.

ROMANS 1:19-20

[19] *For what can be known about God is plain to them, because God has shown it to them.* [20] *For his invisible attributes, namely, his eternal power and divine nature, have been clearly perceived, ever since the creation of the world, in the things that have been made.*

QUESTION 4: How might this passage help us understand what draws people to see natural wonders? List other texts that may help to explain this phenomenon.

Seeing beauty and greatness is one of the passionate desires and deep longings of the human heart—built into us by God. We get pleasure from seeing beauty and greatness in movies and museums and world-class sporting events and art galleries and concerts and the Boundary Waters and the Grand Canyon and the Rockies and the ocean and sunrises and meteor showers. Seeing beauty and greatness is a huge part of our joy in life.

All of these earthly things are images, reflections, pointers to a greater beauty and a greater greatness. They all point to the glory of God. Seeing this will be the end of our quest for beauty and greatness.[3]

DAY 3: GOD'S GREATEST PASSION

QUESTION 5: In your mind, what is uppermost in God's affections? What is his highest priority? Cite Scripture in your answer.

Study the following texts.

PSALM 106:7-8

> [7] *Our fathers, when they were in Egypt, did not consider your wondrous works; they did not remember the abundance of your steadfast love, but rebelled by the sea, at the Red Sea.* [8] *Yet he saved them for his name's sake, that he might make known his mighty power.*

ISAIAH 43:6-7

⁶ *I will say to the north, Give up, and to the south, Do not withhold; bring my sons from afar and my daughters from the end of the earth,* ⁷ *everyone who is called by my name, whom I created for my glory, whom I formed and made.*

ISAIAH 43:25

I, I am he who blots out your transgressions for my own sake, and I will not remember your sins.

ISAIAH 48:9-11

⁹ *For my name's sake I defer my anger, for the sake of my praise I restrain it for you, that I may not cut you off.* ¹⁰ *Behold, I have refined you, but not as silver; I have tried you in the furnace of affliction.* ¹¹ *For my own sake, for my own sake, I do it, for how should my name be profaned? My glory I will not give to another.*

EZEKIEL 36:22-23

²² *Therefore say to the house of Israel, Thus says the Lord GOD: It is not for your sake, O house of Israel, that I am about to act, but for the sake of my holy name, which you have profaned among the nations to which you came.* ²³ *And I will vindicate the holiness of my great name, which has been profaned among the nations, and which you have profaned among them. And the nations will know that I am the LORD, declares the Lord GOD, when through you I vindicate my holiness before their eyes.*

QUESTION 6: Underline every phrase that refers to God's motivation for acting. Summarize the teaching of these verses in your own words.

My conclusion is that God's own glory is uppermost in His own affections. In everything He does, His purpose is to preserve and display that glory. To say that His own glory is uppermost in His own affections means that He puts a greater value on it than on anything else. He delights in His glory above all things.[4]

DAY 4: WHAT IS LOVE?

QUESTION 7: The Bible clearly teaches that "God is love" (1 John 4:8). In today's world, however, *love* is an ambiguous concept. In your own words, attempt to explain what we mean when we say, "God loves us." Be as specific as you can.

I ask people wherever I go: Do you feel loved by God because you believe he makes much of you, or because you believe he frees you and empowers you to enjoy making much of him?[5]

QUESTION 8: Someone might argue that God's consuming passion to magnify his own worth and value is inconsistent with his love for human beings. Attempt to resolve the tension between God's zeal for his supremacy and his love for human beings.

The sad thing is that a radically man-centered view of love permeates our culture and our churches. From the time they can toddle we teach our children that feeling loved means feeling made much of. We have built whole educational philosophies around this view of love—curricula, parenting skills, motivational strategies, therapeutic models, and selling techniques. Most modern people can scarcely imagine an alternative understanding of feeling loved other than feeling made much of. If you don't make much of me you are not loving me.

But when you apply this definition of love to God, it weakens his worth, undermines his goodness, and steals our final satisfaction. . . . This distortion of divine love into an endorsement of self-admiration is subtle. It creeps into our most religious acts. We claim to be praising God because of his love for us. But if his love for us is at bottom his making much of us, who is really being praised? We are willing to be God-centered, it seems, as long as God is man-centered. We are willing to boast in the cross as long as the cross is a witness to our worth. Who then *is* our pride and joy?[6]

DAY 5: SHOULD WE IMITATE GOD?
Read the following passage.

EPHESIANS 5:1

Therefore be imitators of God, as beloved children.

QUESTION 9: We have seen that God does everything for his own glory. In other words, in everything he does, God is self-seeking. In light of this, should we be self-seeking as well? In other words, does the command to imitate God mean that we should seek ourselves in everything that we do? Explain your answer.

Study the following passage.

JOHN 17:24-26

> ^{24} *Father, I desire that they also, whom you have given me, may be with me where I am, to see my glory that you have given me because you loved me before the foundation of the world.* ^{25} *O righteous Father, even though the world does not know you, I know you, and these know that you have sent me.* ^{26} *I made known to them your name, and I will continue to make it known, that the love with which you have loved me may be in them, and I in them.*

QUESTION 10: Is this prayer an expression of Jesus' love for his church? If one of your friends said these exact words to you, would you feel loved by him? Explain your answer.

FURTHER UP AND FURTHER IN

Note: The "Further Up and Further In" section is for those who want to study more. It is a section for further reference and going deeper. The phrase "further up and further in" is borrowed from C. S. Lewis.

Study the following passage.

ROMANS 3:21-26

21 *But now the righteousness of God has been manifested apart from the law, although the Law and the Prophets bear witness to it—* 22 *the righteousness of God through faith in Jesus Christ for all who believe. For there is no distinction:* 23 *for all have sinned and fall short of the glory of God,* 24 *and are justified by his grace as a gift, through the redemption that is in Christ Jesus,* 25 *whom God put forward as a propitiation by his blood, to be received by faith. This was to show God's righteousness, because in his divine forbearance he had passed over former sins.* 26 *It was to show his righteousness at the present time, so that he might be just and the justifier of the one who has faith in Jesus.*

QUESTION 11: According to this text, what was the purpose of the cross? Did Christ die for us or for God? Explain your answer.

Read an article by John Piper entitled "The Goal of God's Love May Not Be What You Think It Is" (you can find it at www.desiringGod.org).

QUESTION 12: What is wrong with viewing love in terms of increasing a person's self-esteem?

QUESTION 13: If you could go to heaven and have all health, all wealth, and all earthly joys, as well as be reunited to all of your loved ones, and yet Christ was not there, would you still want to go? Explain your answer.

Sometimes when people are confronted with the biblical fact that God pursues his own glory in everything he does, they immediately accuse God of being vain. To them it sounds as though God is a very needy person who is trying to be a show-off in order to receive compliments.

QUESTION 14: In light of what you have learned in this lesson, is it right for us to think of God as vain and needy? Why or why not? Cite Scripture in your answer.

Read the following quote from C. S. Lewis.

But the most obvious fact about praise—whether of God or anything—strangely escaped me. I thought of it in terms of compliment, approval, or the giving of honor. I had never noticed that all enjoyment spontaneously overflows into praise unless (sometimes even if) shyness or the fear of boring others is deliberately brought in to check it. The world rings with praise—lovers praising their mistresses, readers their favorite poet, walkers praising the countryside, players praising their favorite game—praise of weather, wines, dishes, actors, horses, colleges, countries, historical personages, children, flowers, mountains, rare stamps, rare beetles, even sometimes politicians and scholars. . . . My whole, more general difficulty about the praise of God depended on my absurdly denying to us, as regards the supremely Valuable, what we delight to do, what indeed we can't help doing, about everything else we value.

I think we delight to praise what we enjoy because the praise not merely expresses, but completes the enjoyment; it is its appointed consummation. It is not out of compliment that lovers keep on telling one another how beautiful they are, the delight is incomplete till it is expressed.[7]

QUESTION 15: According to C. S. Lewis, why is it not vain for God to seek praise from his creatures?

WHILE YOU WATCH THE DVD, TAKE NOTES

What type of person does John Piper have in mind when he is praying and delivering this message?

List the four things that John Piper does not intend to do in these messages.

No one goes to the _____ to increase   .
_____.

We should seek to magnify God like a _____, not like a _____.

What is John Piper's definition of God's love?

AFTER YOU WATCH THE DVD, DISCUSS WHAT YOU'VE LEARNED

1) What is the difference between John Piper's message and the "health, wealth, and prosperity gospel"?

[]

2) Why is the statement "We were created *for the glory of God*" ambiguous? Why is it ambiguous to say that we were created *to magnify God*?

3) How is it loving for God to be self-exalting in everything he does? Does this principle hold true for us as well? Why or why not?

AFTER YOU DISCUSS, MAKE APPLICATION

1) What was the most meaningful part of this lesson for you? Was there a sentence, concept, or idea that really struck you? Why? Record your thoughts in the space below.

2) Devote at least ten minutes this week to meditating on the reality that God created you with the capacity to

marvel at his glory. In the space below, record a time in your life when you experienced this sense of wonder and awe at who God is.

NOTES

1. Excerpt taken from *When I Don't Desire God*, page 14.
2. Excerpt taken from an online article at the Desiring God web site entitled, "Fact! Faith! Feeling!" Throughout this study guide, articles and sermons at the Desiring God web site (www.desiringGod.org) may be found by performing a title search on the home page.
3. Excerpt taken from an online sermon at the Desiring God web site entitled, "Subjected to Futility in Hope, Part 2."
4. Excerpt taken from *Desiring God*, pages 41-42.
5. Excerpt taken from *The Pleasures of God*, page 11.
6. Excerpt taken from *God Is the Gospel*, pages 12-13.
7. Excerpt taken from *Desiring God*, pages 48-49.

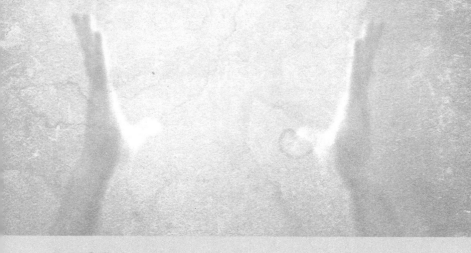

LESSON 3
THE FIGHT FOR JOY IS ESSENTIAL (PART 2)
A Companion Study to the When I Don't Desire God DVD, Session 2

LESSON OBJECTIVES

It is our prayer that after you have finished this lesson . . .

> You will embrace the biblical truth that God is most glorified in you when you are most satisfied in him.

> You will understand how essential the pursuit of joy in God is in the Christian life.

> You will recognize Christian Hedonism as both a liberating and a devastating doctrine.

BEFORE YOU WATCH THE DVD, STUDY AND PREPARE

DAY 1: HOW CAN WE GLORIFY GOD?

QUESTION 1: In the last lesson we saw that we were created to glorify and magnify God. How should we go about fulfilling our purpose? How can we glorify God? Cite Scripture, and be specific in your answer.

Study the following passage.

MATTHEW 13:44

The kingdom of heaven is like treasure hidden in a field, which a man found and covered up. Then in his joy he goes and sells all that he has and buys that field.

Now study the following passage.

MATTHEW 19:24-29

24 *"Again I tell you, it is easier for a camel to go through the eye of a needle than for a rich person to enter the kingdom of God."* 25 *When the disciples heard this, they were greatly astonished, saying, "Who then can be saved?"* 26 *But Jesus looked at them and said, "With man this is impossible, but with God all things are possible."* 27 *Then Peter said in reply, "See, we have left everything and followed you. What then will we have?"* 28 *Jesus said to them, "Truly, I say to you, in the new world, when the Son of Man will sit on his glorious throne, you who have followed me will also sit on twelve thrones, judging the twelve tribes of Israel.* 29 *And everyone who has left houses or brothers or sisters or father or mother or children or lands, for my name's sake, will receive a hundredfold and will inherit eternal life."*

QUESTION 2: Summarize the main point of these two texts in your own words. What do these texts teach us about how we should view self-denial in the Christian life?

DAY 2: TRINITARIAN JOY

Study the following passage.

MATTHEW 3:16-17

¹⁶ And when Jesus was baptized, immediately he went up from the water, and behold, the heavens were opened to him, and he saw the Spirit of God descending like a dove and coming to rest on him; ¹⁷ and behold, a voice from heaven said, "This is my beloved Son, with whom I am well pleased."

Now examine John 3:35 and 5:19-20.

JOHN 3:35

The Father loves the Son and has given all things into his hand.

JOHN 5:19-20

¹⁹ So Jesus said to them, "Truly, truly, I say to you, the Son can do nothing of his own accord, but only what he sees the Father doing. For whatever the Father does, that the Son does likewise. ²⁰ For the Father loves the Son and shows him all that he himself is doing. And greater works than these will he show him, so that you may marvel."

QUESTION 3: From these texts, attempt to describe the relationship between God the Father, God the Son, and God the Holy Spirit.

God is and always has been an exuberantly happy God. From all eternity, even before there were any human beings to love, God has been overflowingly happy in His love for the Son. He has never been lonely. He has always rejoiced, with overflowing satisfaction, in the glory and the partnership of His Son. The Son of God has always been the landscape of God's excellencies and the panorama of God's perfections, so that from all eternity God has beheld, with indescribable satisfaction, the magnificent terrain of His own radiance reflected in the Son.[1]

Study the following texts:

JOHN 15:11

These things I have spoken to you, that my joy may be in you, and that your joy may be full.

JOHN 17:26

I made known to them your name, and I will continue to make it known, that the love with which you have loved me may be in them, and I in them.

QUESTION 4: According to these two texts, why does Jesus make known the name of the Father? Why is this good news for those of us who are dissatisfied with the intensity of our affections for God?

When we share in the happiness of God we share in the very pleasure that the Father has in the Son. This is why Jesus made the Father known to us. . . . He made God known so that God's pleasure in his Son might be in us and become our pleasure.

Imagine being able to enjoy what is most enjoyable with unbounded energy and passion forever. This is not now our experience. . . .

But if the aim of Jesus in John 17:26 comes true, all this will change. If God's pleasure in the Son becomes our pleasure, then the object of our pleasure, Jesus, will be inexhaustible in personal worth. He will never become boring or disappointing or frustrating. No greater treasure can be conceived than the Son of God. Moreover, our ability to savor this inexhaustible treasure will not be limited by human weaknesses. We will enjoy the Son of God with the very enjoyment of his Father. God's delight in his Son will be in us and it will be ours.[2]

DAY 3: DUTY OR DELIGHT?

Study the following texts.

PSALM 37:4

> *Delight yourself in the* LORD, *and he will give you the desires of your heart.*

PSALM 32:11

> *Be glad in the* LORD, *and rejoice, O righteous, and shout for joy, all you upright in heart!*

PHILIPPIANS 4:4

Rejoice in the Lord always; again I will say, Rejoice.

QUESTION 5: In light of these texts, respond to the following statement: "In the Christian life, we should pursue obedience, not joy."

The Bible is full of statements that command us to have certain emotions and affections. From fear (Psalm 2:11; Matthew 10:28) to hope (Psalm 42:5; 1 Peter 1:13) to joy (Psalm 32:11; Romans 12:12) to gratitude (Psalm 100:4; 1 Thessalonians 5:18) to sorrow (Romans 12:15; James 4:9) to love (Deuteronomy 6:5; Romans 12:10), emotions are not just recommended—they are commanded.

QUESTION 6: Reflect on the fact that God commands us to not just perform certain acts but to feel certain emotions. Are you able to order yourself to be happy or feel grateful? What implications does this have for the Christian life? Explain your answer.

We are commanded to feel, not just to think or decide. We are commanded to experience dozens of emotions, not just to perform acts of willpower. . . . I do not believe it is possible to say that Scriptures like these all refer to optional icing on the cake of decision. They are commanded by the Lord who said, "Why do you call me 'Lord, Lord,' and not do what I tell you?" (Luke 6:46).[3]

DAY 4: CHRISTIAN HEDONISM

The theology that is articulated in this study is often called Christian Hedonism. The most concise summary of Christian Hedonism is this: God is most glorified in us when we are most satisfied in him.

QUESTION 7: In your mind, is Christian Hedonism biblical? Explain your answer.

QUESTION 8: How can we square the Bible's emphasis on the necessity of joy in the Christian life with the reality of suffering in the world? Do commands like "Rejoice always" mean that Christians should always smile and be happy?

DAY 5: LIBERATING AND DEVASTATING

John Piper has said that "Christian Hedonism is a liberating and devastating doctrine."[4] The following quotation explains what he means by this.

> When I saw the truth that *God is most glorified in us when we are most satisfied in him,* I was freed from the unbiblical bondage of fear that it was wrong to pursue joy. What once had seemed like an inevitable but defective quest for the satisfaction of my soul now became not just permitted but required. The glory of God was at stake. This was almost too good to be true—that my quest for joy and my duty to glorify God were not in conflict. Indeed they were one. Pursuing joy in God was a nonnegotiable way of honoring God. It was essential. This was a liberating discovery.[5]

QUESTION 9: Why is Christian Hedonism a liberating doctrine? Have you personally experienced Christian Hedonism to be liberating in the way that John Piper describes?

> This discovery was devastating to me. It still is. I was made to know and enjoy God. I was freed by the doctrine of Christian Hedonism to pursue that knowledge and that joy with all my heart. And then, to my dismay, I discovered that it is not an easy doctrine. Christian Hedonism is not a lowering of the bar. Out of the blue, as it were, I realized that the bar had been raised. Manageable, duty-defined, decision-oriented, willpower Christianity now seemed easy, and

real Christianity had become impossible. The emotions—
or affections, as former generations called them—which I
was now free to enjoy, proved to be beyond my reach. The
Christian life became impossible.[6]

QUESTION 10: Explain how Christian Hedonism is a raising of the bar. Why is raising the bar in this way a devastating truth?

FURTHER UP AND FURTHER IN

Read the sermon entitled "Worship: The Feast of Christian Hedonism" (www.desiringGod.org).

QUESTION 11: List the three ways that the heart can respond in worship to God. What are the differences between these three ways?

QUESTION 12: Respond to this objection: "Christian Hedonism makes a god out of pleasure."

QUESTION 13: If persons claim to be committed to God while their heart is in love with money, food, or sex, is God honored in their lives? Can they rightly claim to be Christians? Why or why not?

When speaking of the pursuit of joy, we Christian Hedonists can sometimes give the false impression that what we are really after is a psychological experience of happiness without any regard to what makes us happy. C. S. Lewis helps us to avoid this danger in the following quotation.

> You cannot hope and also think about hoping at the same moment; for in hope we look to hope's object and we interrupt this by (so to speak) turning round to look at the hope itself. . . . The surest means of disarming an anger or a lust was to turn your attention from the girl or the insult and start examining the passion itself. The surest way of spoiling a pleasure was to start examining your satisfaction. . . .
>
> I perceived (and this was the wonder of wonders) that . . . I had been equally wrong in supposing that I desired Joy itself. Joy itself, considered simply as an event in my own mind, turned out to be of no value at all. All the value lay in that of which Joy was the desiring. And that object, quite clearly, was no state of my own mind or body at all. . . . I asked if Joy itself was what I wanted; and, labeling it "aesthetic experience," had pretended I could answer Yes. But that answer too had broken down. Inexorably Joy pro-

claimed, "You want—I myself am your want of—something other, outside, not you nor any state of you."[7]

QUESTION 14: Why are the experience of satisfaction and the contemplation of satisfaction mutually exclusive activities? If Lewis is correct, then how should we pursue joy?

QUESTION 15: Why is it important to emphasize that we must pursue *joy* in God rather than simply saying that we should pursue God?

WHILE YOU WATCH THE DVD, TAKE NOTES

When God is our _____ _____, we display him as our _____ _____.

How does John Piper respond to the objection that we should talk about serving Jesus instead of joy?

The aim is not to _____ _____, but to _____
_____.

What is the most common question John Piper has received in the past twenty years?

Why does John Piper believe that we should emphasize the need to pursue *joy* in God rather than simply the need to pursue God?

AFTER YOU WATCH THE DVD, DISCUSS WHAT YOU'VE LEARNED

1) Discuss the ways in which Christian Hedonism is both a liberating doctrine and a devastating doctrine.

2) How does the pursuit of joy in God relate to the call for risk-taking, sacrificial love?

3) Should people who don't experience delight in God fear that they are not saved? Why or why not?

AFTER YOU DISCUSS, MAKE APPLICATION

1) What was the most meaningful part of this lesson for you? Was there a sentence, concept, or idea that really struck you? Why? Record your thoughts in the space below.

2) C. S. Lewis argued that you can't pursue joy directly. Meditate on how you can pursue joy in God indirectly. Come up with three ways to do so, and seek to practice them in your life this week.

NOTES

1. Excerpt taken from *The Pleasures of God*, page 48.
2. Excerpt taken from *The Pleasures of God*, pages 26-27.
3. Excerpt taken from *Desiring God*, page 300.
4. Excerpt taken from *When I Don't Desire God*, page 13.
5. Excerpt taken from *When I Don't Desire God*, page 13.
6. Excerpt taken from *When I Don't Desire God*, page 14.
7. Excerpt taken from *When I Don't Desire God*, page 30.

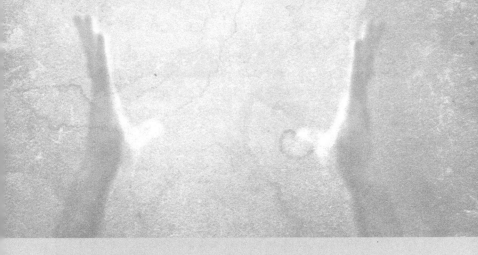

LESSON 4
HOW TO FIGHT AND WHAT TO FIGHT FOR (PART 1)
A Companion Study to the When I Don't Desire God DVD, Session 3

LESSON OBJECTIVES

It is our prayer that after you have finished this lesson . . .

> You will recognize the profound and radical nature of your own sinfulness.

> You will embrace the truth that joy in God is a sovereign gift from God.

> You will acknowledge that an essential element of saving faith is delight in the glory of God.

BEFORE YOU WATCH THE DVD, STUDY AND PREPARE

DAY 1: JOY IN GOD IS A GIFT FROM GOD

In this session John Piper will argue that joy in God is both a gift from God and something that we must fight for. Read the following quotation from John Piper on Jesus' encounter with the rich young ruler.

When the rich young ruler walked away from Jesus because he delighted more in his riches than in following Christ, Jesus said, "It is easier for a camel to go through the eye of a needle than for a rich person to enter the kingdom of God" (Matt. 19:24). The disciples were astonished at this. They knew that a camel *cannot* go through the eye of a needle. That's true. And humans cannot make themselves delight in Christ more than money. So Jesus answered, "With man this is impossible, but with God all things are possible" (v. 26). . . . This was Jesus' way of saying that joy in God is a gift. Preferring Jesus to money is a gift of God. We can't produce it on our own. It must be given to us.[1]

Study Galatians 5:22-23 and Romans 15:13.

GALATIANS 5:22-23

[22] *But the fruit of the Spirit is love, joy, peace, patience, kindness, goodness, faithfulness,* [23] *gentleness, self-control; against such things there is no law.*

ROMANS 15:13

May the God of hope fill you with all joy and peace in believing, so that by the power of the Holy Spirit you may abound in hope.

QUESTION 1: How do these two texts confirm the truth that joy in God is a gift from God?

QUESTION 2: What other evidence can you give that indicates that joy in God is a gift from God? If joy is a gift from God, then what is our responsibility in the fight for joy?

DAY 2: RADICAL CORRUPTION

The Bible is not optimistic about human nature. In fact, the Bible continually portrays human beings as totally fallen, utterly sinful, and radically corrupt.

Study the following texts on the extent of human sinfulness.

GENESIS 6:5

The LORD saw that the wickedness of man was great in the earth, and that every intention of the thoughts of his heart was only evil continually.

JEREMIAH 17:9

The heart is deceitful above all things, and desperately sick; who can understand it?

JOHN 8:34

Jesus answered them, "Truly, truly, I say to you, everyone who commits sin is a slave to sin."

EPHESIANS 2:1-3

¹ And you were dead in the trespasses and sins ² in which you once walked, following the course of this world, following the prince of the power of the air, the spirit that is now at work in the sons of disobedience— ³ among whom we all once lived in the passions of our flesh, carrying out the desires of the body and the mind, and were by nature children of wrath, like the rest of mankind.

2 CORINTHIANS 4:3-4

³ And even if our gospel is veiled, it is veiled only to those who are perishing. ⁴ In their case the god of this world has blinded the minds of the unbelievers, to keep them from seeing the light of the gospel of the glory of Christ, who is the image of God.

QUESTION 3: Summarize the teaching of these passages. List the different ways that human sinfulness is described. What do these texts teach us about our ability to delight in God?

Study the following passage.

JOHN 3:19-20

¹⁹ And this is the judgment: the light has come into the world, and people loved the darkness rather than the light because their deeds were evil. ²⁰ For everyone who does wicked things hates the light and does not come to the light, lest his deeds should be exposed.

QUESTION 4: What is the natural response of human beings to divine light? What must happen if human beings are ever to come to the light?

The deepest reason why we cannot rejoice in the Lord is that by nature we are dead. That is, we have no spiritual sensitivity to the truth and beauty of the gospel of Christ. We are like the blind in the art gallery of heaven. Our deadness is not the deadness of the body. It's not even the deadness of the intellect or the will. It is the deadness of the spiritual ability to see reality for what it is. . . . Because of this fallen, sinful, hardened, rebellious, futile, dead condition of our hearts, joy in God is impossible. Not impossible in a way that makes us less guilty, but more guilty.[2]

DAY 3: COMMANDING THE IMPOSSIBLE

Study the following passage.

ROMANS 8:5-8

> [5] *For those who live according to the flesh set their minds on the things of the flesh, but those who live according to the Spirit set their minds on the things of the Spirit.* [6] *For to set the mind on the flesh is death, but to set the mind on the Spirit is life and peace.* [7] *For the mind that is set on the flesh is hostile to God, for it does not submit to God's law; indeed, it cannot.* [8] *Those who are in the flesh cannot please God.*

QUESTION 5: Does the fact that human beings in the flesh *cannot* submit to God's law remove their responsibility to obey God? In other words, can God condemn us for not doing something that we are unable to do? Explain your answer.

QUESTION 6: Interact with the following statement: "Joy in God must be something that we can control because God commands it."

God has the right to command of you what you cannot turn on and off with a spigot. . . . God can command of me what I ought to give even if, by virtue of my profound rebellion and corruption, I can't give it until I am born of God and transformed from within.[3]

DAY 4: WHAT IS FAITH?
Study John 6:35 and Hebrews 11:6.

JOHN 6:35

Jesus said to them, "I am the bread of life; whoever comes to me shall not hunger, and whoever believes in me shall never thirst."

HEBREWS 11:6

And without faith it is impossible to please him, for whoever would draw near to God must believe that he exists and that he rewards those who seek him.

QUESTION 7: From these texts, derive a definition of faith. How does faith relate to longing and desire?

Study the following passage.

JAMES 2:19

You believe that God is one; you do well. Even the demons believe—and shudder!

QUESTION 8: What is the difference between the faith of demons and the faith of Christians? Is it possible to have genuine faith and yet not have any affections for God?

In all the acts of saving faith, the Holy Spirit enables us not just to perceive and affirm factual truth, but also to apprehend and embrace spiritual beauty. It is the "embracing of spiritual beauty" that is the essential core of saving faith.

This is what I mean by "being satisfied with all that God is for us in Jesus." Spiritual beauty is the beauty of God diffused in all his works and words. Embracing this, or delighting in it, or being satisfied with it, is the heart of saving faith.[4]

DAY 5: GLORIOUS MYSTERY

The following quotation from John Piper summarizes the central mystery of the Christian life that we have seen in this lesson.

We are commanded to do what we cannot do. And we must do it or perish. Our inability does not remove our guilt—it deepens it. We are so bad that we cannot love God. We cannot delight in God above all things. We cannot treasure Christ above money. Our entrenched badness does not make it wrong for God to command us to be good. We ought to delight in God above all things. Therefore it is right for God to command us to delight in God above all things. And if we ever do delight in God, it will be because we have obeyed this command.

That is the mystery: We must obey the command to rejoice in the Lord, and we cannot, because of our willful and culpable corruption. Therefore obedience, when it happens, is a gift. The heretic Pelagius in the fourth century rejected this truth and was shocked and angered when he saw the way St. Augustine prayed in his *Confessions*. Augustine prayed, "Give me the grace [O Lord] to do as you command, and command me to do what you will! . . . O holy God . . . when your commands are obeyed, it is from you that we receive the power to obey them."[5]

QUESTION 9: In your own words, summarize the central mystery of the Christian life that is outlined in this lesson.

QUESTION 10: What is your reaction to Augustine's prayer? Do you think it is a biblical prayer? Cite Scripture in your answer.

FURTHER UP AND FURTHER IN
Study the following passage.

JEREMIAH 2:12-13

> [12] *Be appalled, O heavens, at this; be shocked, be utterly desolate, declares the LORD,* [13] *for my people have committed two evils: they have forsaken me, the fountain of living waters, and hewed out cisterns for themselves, broken cisterns that can hold no water.*

QUESTION 11: According to this text, what is so shocking about evil? What would be the opposite of evil in this passage?

God pictures himself as a mountain spring of clean, cool, life-giving water. The way to glorify a fountain like this is to enjoy the water, praise the water, and keep coming back to the water, and point other people to the water, and get strength for love from the water, and never, never, never prefer any drink in the world over this water. That makes the spring look valuable. That is how we glorify God, the fountain of living water.

But in Jeremiah's day people tasted the fountain of God's grace and did not like it. . . . They put God's perfections to the tongue of their souls and disliked what they tasted; then they turned and craved the suicidal cisterns of the world. That double insult to God is the essence of what evil is.[6]

Read a sermon by John Piper entitled "Why We Need a Savior: Dead in Sins" (www.desiringGod.org).

QUESTION 12: In light of our natural sinfulness, in what two ways is conversion described in Ephesians 2:1-10?

Study Acts 16:31 and Philippians 1:29.

ACTS 16:31

And they said, "Believe in the Lord Jesus, and you will be saved, you and your household."

PHILIPPIANS 1:29

For it has been granted to you that for the sake of Christ you should not only believe in him but also suffer for his sake.

Now study Acts 2:37-38 and 2 Timothy 2:24-26.

Lesson 4

ACTS 2:37-38

> ³⁷ Now when they heard this they were cut to the heart, and said to Peter and the rest of the apostles, "Brothers, what shall we do?" ³⁸ And Peter said to them, "Repent and be baptized every one of you in the name of Jesus Christ for the forgiveness of your sins, and you will receive the gift of the Holy Spirit."

2 TIMOTHY 2:24-26

> ²⁴ And the Lord's servant must not be quarrelsome but kind to everyone, able to teach, patiently enduring evil, ²⁵ correcting his opponents with gentleness. God may perhaps grant them repentance leading to a knowledge of the truth, ²⁶ and they may come to their senses and escape from the snare of the devil, after being captured by him to do his will.

Finally, examine Philippians 2:12-13.

PHILIPPIANS 2:12-13

> ¹² Therefore, my beloved, as you have always obeyed, so now, not only as in my presence but much more in my absence, work out your own salvation with fear and trembling, ¹³ for it is God who works in you, both to will and to work for his good pleasure.

QUESTION 13: From your study of these texts, should we view faith, repentance, and working out our salvation as divine gifts or human responsibilities? Whose action is more fundamental—God's or man's?

Throughout these lessons, you have learned that the fight for joy is a very serious fight. The following quotation from John Piper clarifies what is at stake.

> A person who has no taste for the enjoyment of Christ will not go to heaven. "If anyone has no love for the Lord, let him be accursed" (1 Cor. 16:22). "Whoever loves father or mother more than me is not worthy of me, and whoever loves son or daughter more than me is not worthy of me" (Matt. 10:37). "Though you have not seen him, you love him. Though you do not now see him, you believe in him and rejoice with joy that is inexpressible and filled with glory" (1 Pet. 1:8). Loving Jesus, not just "deciding" for him or "being committed to him" or affirming all the right doctrines about him, is the mark of a true child of God. Jesus said, "If God were your Father, you would love me" (John 8:42). . . . Surely, then, this is worth fighting for. It may feel strange at first, but when we see what is at stake, no battle will seem more important. Loving Christ involves delight in his Person. Without this love no one goes to heaven. Therefore there is no more important struggle in the universe than the struggle to see and savor Christ above all things—the struggle for joy.[7]

QUESTION 14: Has Piper correctly understood the texts that he cites? What is your reaction to statements like "A person who has no taste for the enjoyment of Christ will not go to heaven"?

Read a sermon by John Piper entitled "God's Great Mercy and the New Birth" (www.desiringGod.org).

QUESTION 15: Summarize Piper's description of the New Testament picture of our new birth. What can you conclude about the sovereignty of God in salvation?

WHILE YOU WATCH THE DVD, TAKE NOTES

_____ _____ would be a good bumper sticker.

What is John Piper's definition of faith?

What two mistakes do people often make in trying to put the fight for joy and the spontaneity of joy together?

How is our fight for joy like a farmer seeking to grow crops?

List the four things that modesty accomplishes in the fight for joy:

1.

2.

3.

4.

AFTER YOU WATCH THE DVD, DISCUSS WHAT YOU'VE LEARNED

1) In light of what you've learned, how should we balance the truths that joy is a spontaneous gift from God and that joy is something for which we must fight?

2) Explain why the truth that repentance is a gift of God does not undercut evangelism but actually empowers evangelism.

3) Discuss the ways that believing in the sovereign grace of God produces modesty in our fight for joy.

AFTER YOU DISCUSS, MAKE APPLICATION

1) What was the most meaningful part of this lesson for you? Was there a sentence, concept, or idea that really struck you? Why? Record your thoughts in the space below.

2) Reflect on ways that you have been presumptuous in the Christian life. In what areas of your life have you assumed that ultimate determination is up to you? Take some time this week to think about this and to repent of any presumption in your walk with Christ.

NOTES

1. Excerpt taken from *When I Don't Desire God*, page 50.
2. Excerpt taken from *When I Don't Desire God*, pages 49-50.
3. Excerpt taken from audio sermon at the Desiring God web site entitled, "Christian Hedonism Unpacked."
4. Excerpt taken from *Future Grace*, page 206.
5. Excerpt taken from *When I Don't Desire God*, page 53.
6. Excerpt taken from *When I Don't Desire God*, pages 33-34.
7. Excerpt taken from *When I Don't Desire God*, pages 34-35.

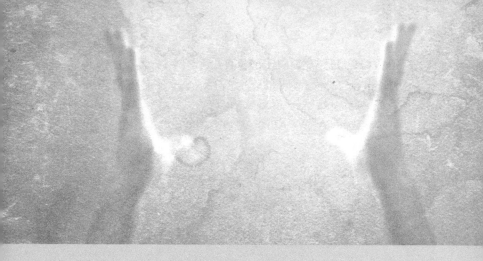

LESSON 5
HOW TO FIGHT AND WHAT TO FIGHT FOR (PART 2)
A Companion Study to the When I Don't Desire God DVD, Session 4

LESSON OBJECTIVES

It is our prayer that after you have finished this lesson . . .

> You will understand the crucial distinction between justification and sanctification.

> You will learn the secret of "gutsy guilt."

> The eyes of your heart will have been opened by God to see and savor him in new ways.

BEFORE YOU WATCH THE DVD, STUDY AND PREPARE

DAY 1: JUSTIFICATION BY FAITH

The doctrine of justification by faith is one of the central truths of the Christian faith.

> The doctrine of justification says that the remedy for my alienation from God is first a legal one, and only then a moral one. First, I have to be legally absolved of guilt and

credited with a righteousness that I don't have. That is, I have to be declared righteous in the courtroom of heaven, where God sits as judge, and where I stand condemned by his law. That's what the word *justify* means: not *make* just, but *declare* just.[1]

Study Galatians 2:16, Romans 3:28, and Romans 4:4-8.

GALATIANS 2:16

Yet we know that a person is not justified by works of the law but through faith in Jesus Christ, so we also have believed in Christ Jesus, in order to be justified by faith in Christ and not by works of the law, because by works of the law no one will be justified.

ROMANS 3:28

For we hold that one is justified by faith apart from works of the law.

ROMANS 4:4-8

[4] *Now to the one who works, his wages are not counted as a gift but as his due.* [5] *And to the one who does not work but trusts him who justifies the ungodly, his faith is counted as righteousness,* [6] *just as David also speaks of the blessing of the one to whom God counts righteousness apart from works:* [7] *"Blessed are those whose lawless deeds are forgiven, and whose sins are covered;* [8] *blessed is the man against whom the Lord will not count his sin."*

QUESTION 1: What are the two possible ways that human beings can be declared righteous before God in these passages? Why do you think Paul rejects justification by works?

Study the following passage.

ROMANS 8:31-34

> [31] *What then shall we say to these things? If God is for us, who can be against us?* [32] *He who did not spare his own Son but gave him up for us all, how will he not also with him graciously give us all things?* [33] *Who shall bring any charge against God's elect? It is God who justifies.* [34] *Who is to condemn? Christ Jesus is the one who died—more than that, who was raised—who is at the right hand of God, who indeed is interceding for us.*

QUESTION 2: How is God able to "justify the ungodly" (Romans 4:5)? What is the ultimate reason that God can be completely for us?

DAY 2: SANCTIFICATION

The following quotation from John Piper describes what happens after a person is justified by faith.

> Then, and only then, on the basis of this forgiveness and this declaration of righteousness, God gives us his Holy Spirit to transform us morally and progressively into the image of his Son. This progressive change is *not* justification but is based on justification. This change is what we call *sanctification*.[2]

Study the following passage.

EPHESIANS 2:8-10

> *8 For by grace you have been saved through faith. And this is not your own doing; it is the gift of God, 9 not a result of works, so that no one may boast. 10 For we are his workmanship, created in Christ Jesus for good works, which God prepared before-hand, that we should walk in them.*

QUESTION 3: Why is it necessary for salvation to come by grace through faith? Does salvation by grace undercut the necessity of good works? Why or why not?

One way to conceive of the relationship between justification and sanctification is this: We are accepted by God (justification); therefore, we obey God (sanctification).

QUESTION 4: Why is it vital that we preserve the proper order of justification and sanctification? What would be the result if we inverted the order?

Both [justification and sanctification] are gifts, and both are bought by the blood of Christ. They are inseparable but different. Both are by faith alone. Justification is by faith alone because only faith receives the declaration that the ungodly is counted righteous. Sanctification is by faith alone because only faith receives the power to bear the fruit of love. It is crucial in the fight for joy that we not confuse or combine justification and sanctification. Confusing them will, in the end, undermine the gospel and turn justification by *faith* into justification by *performance*. If that happens, the great gospel weapon in the fight for joy will fall from our hands.[3]

DAY 3: INTRODUCING GUTSY GUILT

Study the following passage.

MICAH 7:8-9

[8] *Rejoice not over me, O my enemy; when I fall, I shall rise; when I sit in darkness, the LORD will be a light to me.* [9] *I will bear the indignation of the LORD because I have sinned against him, until he pleads my cause and executes judgment for me. He will bring me out to the light; I shall look upon his vindication.*

QUESTION 5: What is shocking about Micah's confidence in God's favor in this passage?

QUESTION 6: John Piper refers to Micah's attitude in this passage as "gutsy guilt."[4] What do you think this phrase means?

DAY 4: TWO WAYS TO SEE

Study the following passage.

MATTHEW 13:13-15

> *13 This is why I speak to them in parables, because seeing they do not see, and hearing they do not hear, nor do they understand. 14 Indeed, in their case the prophecy of Isaiah is fulfilled that says: "You will indeed hear but never understand, and you will indeed see but never perceive. 15 For this people's heart has grown dull, and with their ears they can barely hear, and their eyes they have closed, lest they should see with their eyes and hear with their ears and understand with their heart and turn, and I would heal them."*

QUESTION 7: This passage refers to two different types of sight and hearing. What is the difference between these two types of sight and hearing?

Study the following passage.

2 CORINTHIANS 4:4-6

> *4 In their case the god of this world has blinded the minds of the unbelievers, to keep them from seeing the light of the gospel of the glory of Christ, who is the image of God. 5 For what we proclaim is not ourselves, but Jesus Christ as Lord, with ourselves as your servants for Jesus' sake. 6 For God, who said, "Let light shine out of darkness," has shone in our hearts to give the light of the knowledge of the glory of God in the face of Jesus Christ.*

QUESTION 8: In this passage, what does Satan prevent unbelievers from seeing? What is God's solution to this blindness? Do believers still struggle to "see" in this way?

DAY 5: BEHOLDING AND BECOMING

Study the following passage.

2 CORINTHIANS 4:16-18

[16] *So we do not lose heart. Though our outer nature is wasting away, our inner nature is being renewed day by day.* [17] *For this light momentary affliction is preparing for us an eternal weight of glory beyond all comparison,* [18] *as we look not to the things that are seen but to the things that are unseen. For the things that are seen are transient, but the things that are unseen are eternal.*

QUESTION 9: According to this passage, how is our inner nature renewed every day? If the things that we look to are unseen, where do we look for them? What do we look at?

Study the following passage.

2 CORINTHIANS 3:18

And we all, with unveiled face, beholding the glory of the Lord, are being transformed into the same image from one degree of glory to another. For this comes from the Lord who is the Spirit.

QUESTION 10: According to this text, how are we transformed into the image of Christ? Do you think that "beholding" refers to mere observation or to something more? To what else might it refer?

What is this internal change that comes from "beholding the glory of the Lord"?

It is the awakening of a new taste for spiritual reality centering in Christ. It is the capacity for a new sweetness and a new enjoyment of the glory of God in the Word of God. Therefore, nothing is more important for us in life than to "behold the glory of the Lord."[5]

FURTHER UP AND FURTHER IN

Read the following statement on "God's Work in Faith and Sanctification" from section 10.1 of "The Desiring God Affirmation of Faith":

We believe that justification and sanctification are both brought about by God through faith, but not in the same way. Justification is an act of God's imputing and reckoning;

sanctification is an act of God's imparting and transforming. Thus the function of faith in regard to each is different. In regard to justification, faith is not the channel through which power or transformation flows to the soul of the believer, but rather faith is the occasion of God's forgiving, acquitting, and reckoning as righteous. But in regard to sanctification, faith is indeed the channel through which divine power and transformation flow to the soul; and the sanctifying work of God through faith does indeed touch the soul and change it into the likeness of Christ.[6]

QUESTION 11: In your own words, what is the crucial difference between how faith functions in justification and sanctification? Why is this distinction so important? What happens if we lose this distinction?

The following lyrics by Charitie Lees Bancroft beautifully celebrate the doctrine of justification by faith. The song is entitled "Before the Throne of God Above."

Before the throne of God above
I have a strong and perfect plea
A great High Priest whose name is love
Who ever lives and pleads for me
My name is graven on His hands
My name is written on His heart
I know that while in heaven He stands
No tongue can bid me thence depart
No tongue can bid me thence depart

When Satan tempts me to despair
And tells me of the guilt within
Upward I look and see Him there
Who made an end of all my sin
Because the sinless Savior died
My sinful soul is counted free
For God, the Just, is satisfied
To look on Him and pardon me
To look on Him and pardon me

Behold Him there! The risen Lamb
My perfect, spotless Righteousness
The great unchangeable I AM
The King of Glory and of Grace
One with Himself I cannot die
My soul is purchased by His blood
My life is hid with Christ on high
With Christ, my Savior and my God
With Christ, my Savior and my God.[7]

QUESTION 12: How does this song celebrate the doctrine of justification by faith alone?

QUESTION 13: How does this song exemplify "gutsy guilt?"

In the following quotation, John Piper describes what it means to see with the eyes of the heart.

> What then is this seeing with the eyes of the heart? It is a spiritual perception of the truth and beauty and worth of Christ for what they really are. To use the words of Jonathan Edwards, it is "a true sense of the divine excellency of the things revealed in the Word of God, and a conviction of the truth a reality of them thence arising." The key word is "sense." The person who sees with the eyes of the heart "does not merely rationally believe that God is glorious, but he has a *sense* of the gloriousness of God in his heart. There is not only a rational belief that God is holy, and that holiness is a good thing, but there is a sense of the loveliness of God's holiness."[8]

QUESTION 14: In your own words, define what it means to see with the eyes of the heart. How does this spiritual sight relate to physical sight?

Read the following quote from Jonathan Edwards.

> There is a difference between having a rational judgment that honey is sweet, and having a sense of its sweetness. A man may have the former, that knows not how honey tastes; but a man cannot have the latter unless he has an idea of the taste of honey in his mind. So there is a difference between believing that a person is beautiful, and having a

sense of his beauty. The former may be obtained by hear-say, but the latter only by seeing the countenance. There is a wide difference between mere speculative rational judging any thing to be excellent, and having a sense of its sweet-ness and beauty. The former rests only in the head, specu-lation only is concerned in it; but the heart is concerned in the latter. When the heart is sensible of the beauty and amiableness of a thing, it necessarily feels pleasure in the apprehension. It is implied in a person's being heartily sensible of the loveliness of a thing, that the idea of it is sweet and pleasant to his soul; which is a far different thing from having a rational opinion that it is excellent.[9]

QUESTION 15: What is the difference between a rational judgment about the sweetness of honey and a sense of the sweetness of honey? How can you acquire each type of knowledge?

WHILE YOU WATCH THE DVD, TAKE NOTES

We do not _____ in order to be _____. We _____ as _____ _____.

What is the only type of sin that we are able to defeat?

What is the main fight in the Christian life?

Where do we see the glory of God?

1.

2.

According to John Piper, why is the universe so big?

AFTER YOU WATCH THE DVD, DISCUSS WHAT YOU'VE LEARNED

1) Why is it disastrous to confuse justification and sanctification? What is the practical effect of confusing these two doctrines?

2) What is "gutsy guilt," and how is it manifested in the Christian life?

3) Discuss what it means to "see and savor the glory of God."

AFTER YOU DISCUSS, MAKE APPLICATION

1) What was the most meaningful part of this lesson for you? Was there a sentence, concept, or idea that really struck you? Why? Record your thoughts in the space below.

2) Memorize Micah 7:7-8 this week. Share the secret of gutsy guilt with a fellow believer who is struggling with guilt over his or her sin.

NOTES

1. Excerpt taken from *When I Don't Desire God*, page 82.
2. Excerpt taken from *When I Don't Desire God*, page 84.
3. Excerpt taken from *When I Don't Desire God*, page 84.

4. Phrase taken from *When I Don't Desire God*, page 87.

5. Excerpt taken from *When I Don't Desire God*, page 66.

6. Excerpt taken from http://www.desiringGod.org/media/pdf/affirmation_of_faith.pdf.

7. This hymn is in public domain.

8. Excerpt taken from *When I Don't Desire God*, pages 67-68.

9. Excerpt taken from a sermon by Jonathan Edwards entitled "A Divine and Supernatural Light." This sermon may be found in *The Works of Jonathan Edwards*, Vol. 2 (Peabody, MA: Hendrickson, 1998).

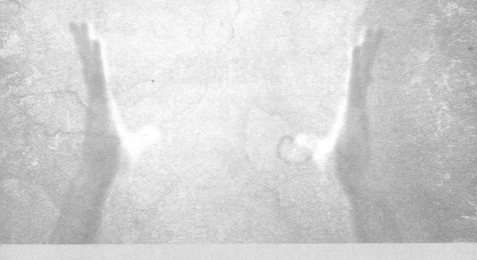

LESSON 6
STRATEGIES FOR THE FIGHT (PART 1)
A Companion Study to the When I Don't Desire God DVD, Session 5

LESSON OBJECTIVES

It is our prayer that after you have finished this lesson . . .

> You will begin to wield the Word of God in the fight for joy.

> You will have a better understanding of what to look for when you read the Word of God.

> You will begin to pray earnestly and continually for everything you need to be happy in God.

BEFORE YOU WATCH THE DVD, STUDY AND PREPARE

DAY 1: THE WORD OF GOD IN THE FIGHT FOR JOY

The final two lessons will seek to draw out practical ways to fight for joy. The first and most fundamental weapon in our fight for joy is the Word of God. John Piper explains this important point.

The fundamental reason that the Word of God is essential to joy in God is that God reveals *himself* mainly by his Word. And seeing this revelation of God is the foundation of our joy. . . . Oh how precious is the Bible! Here is where we see God most clearly and most surely. The Holy Spirit opens our eyes and grants us to see the beauty of Christ (Matt. 16:17; Acts 16:14). If there were no Bible, there would be no lasting joy. . . . We need the Word of God not only to see God in the Word, but to see him rightly anywhere else.[1]

Study Matthew 4:3-4, Romans 15:4, Galatians 3:5, and John 15:7.

MATTHEW 4:3-4

3 And the tempter came and said to him, "If you are the Son of God, command these stones to become loaves of bread." 4 But he answered, "It is written, 'Man shall not live by bread alone, but by every word that comes from the mouth of God.'"

ROMANS 15:4

For whatever was written in former days was written for our instruction, that through endurance and through the encouragement of the Scriptures we might have hope.

GALATIANS 3:5

Does he who supplies the Spirit to you and works miracles among you do so by works of the law, or by hearing with faith?

JOHN 15:7

> *If you abide in me, and my words abide in you, ask whatever you wish, and it will be done for you.*

QUESTION 1: For each of the texts above, list the purpose or function of the Word of God.

Study the following passage.

PSALM 19:7-11

> 7 *The law of the* LORD *is perfect, reviving the soul; the testimony of the* LORD *is sure, making wise the simple;* 8 *the precepts of the* LORD *are right, rejoicing the heart; the commandment of the* LORD *is pure, enlightening the eyes;* 9 *the fear of the* LORD *is clean, enduring forever; the rules of the* LORD *are true, and righteous altogether.* 10 *More to be desired are they than gold, even much fine gold; sweeter also than honey and drippings of the honeycomb.* 11 *Moreover, by them is your servant warned; in keeping them there is great reward.*

QUESTION 2: Circle every adjective that describes the Word of God. Underline every phrase that describes the function of the Word of God. Spend five minutes meditating on the implications of this passage for your reading of Scripture. Record your observations below.

DAY 2: THE SWORD OF THE SPIRIT AND THE DECEITFULNESS OF SIN

Examine Ephesians 4:22 and Romans 7:11.

EPHESIANS 4:22

Put off your old self, which belongs to your former manner of life and is corrupt through deceitful desires.

ROMANS 7:11

For sin, seizing an opportunity through the commandment, deceived me and through it killed me.

Both of these texts indicate that the power of sin lies in its ability to deceive us. As John Piper says:

"Deceitful desires" can trick us into feeling that sinful thoughts and acts will be more satisfying than seeing God. The illusion is so strong it creates moral confusion, so that people find ways to justify sin as good, or, if not good, at least permissible.[2]

QUESTION 3: For each of the sins listed below, explain how deceitful desires helped to produce the sinful act.

1) A young student treats his classmates with contempt in order to impress some older students.

2) A wife abandons her husband in order to have a relationship with another man.

3) A child throws a temper tantrum because his mother refuses to buy him a new toy.

4) A man who just lost his job cuts corners on his tax return.

Ephesians 6:11-18 describes the armor of God that believers should wear in order to make war on sin. The only offensive weapon mentioned is "the sword of the Spirit, which is the word of God" (6:17). So the Word of God is our weapon of choice with which we can combat the deceitful desires of sin.

The power of sin is the promise of deceitful desires? Then we will match promise for promise! Go ahead, sin, put up your best promises! We will put God's promises against yours. Nothing—nothing in this world—can surpass in value and depth and height and durability the pleasure that God promises.[3]

QUESTION 4: For each of the examples from Question 3, find one passage of Scripture that exposes the deceitful desire and offers an alternative and superior satisfaction. (Hint: use a concordance if you have trouble thinking of a passage.)

DAY 3: MEDITATING DAY AND NIGHT
Study Joshua 1:8, Psalm 1:1-2, Psalm 119:97, Psalm 143:5.

JOSHUA 1:8

This Book of the Law shall not depart from your mouth, but you shall meditate on it day and night, so that you may be careful to do according to all that is written in it. For then you will make your way prosperous, and then you will have good success.

PSALM 1:1-2

[1] Blessed is the man who walks not in the counsel of the wicked, nor stands in the way of sinners, nor sits in the seat of scoffers; [2] but his delight is in the law of the LORD, and on his law he meditates day and night.

PSALM 119:97

Oh how I love your law! It is my meditation all the day.

PSALM 143:5

*I remember the days of old; I meditate on all that you have done;
I ponder the work of your hands.*

QUESTION 5: What does it mean to meditate on the
Scriptures? How does that differ from normal reading?

> Meditating on the Word of God day and night means to
> speak to yourself the Word of God day and night and to
> speak to yourself about it—to mull it over, to ask questions
> about it and answer them from the Scripture itself, to ask
> yourself how this might apply to you and others, and to
> ponder its implications for life and church and culture and
> missions.[4]

In addition to the Word of God, prayer is essential in the fight
for joy. In the following passage, John Piper explains the insepara-
bility of prayer and meditation.

> Prayer and meditation are inseparable in the fight for joy. This
> inseparability is rooted in God's design to make the Spirit of
> God and the Word of God inseparable. His purpose for our

lives is that the work of his Spirit happen through his Word, and that the work of his Word happen through his Spirit. . . .

Prayer and meditation correspond to God's Spirit and God's Word. *Prayer* is our response to God in reliance on his Spirit; and *meditation* is our response to God in reliance on his Word.

In *prayer* we praise the perfections of God through his Spirit, we thank God for what he has done by his Spirit, we confess our failures to trust the promise of his Spirit, and we ask for the help of his Spirit—all in Jesus' name. Prayer is the human expression of treasuring and trusting the Spirit of God.

In *meditation*, as the counterpart to prayer, we hear and ponder and prize the Word of God. Meditation means reading the Bible and chewing on it to get the sweetness and the nourishment from it that God designs to give. . . . This is how the Word serves joy.[5]

QUESTION 6: Describe in your own words the relationship between prayer and the Word of God. What happens if you try to separate the Word of God from prayer?

DAY 4: WHAT ARE WE SEARCHING FOR?

We have seen that thinking, meditating, and searching the Scriptures is essential in the fight for joy. But when we go to the Scriptures, what are we looking for?

Examine John 5:39 and Luke 24:27.

JOHN 5:39

You search the Scriptures because you think that in them you have eternal life; and it is they that bear witness about me.

LUKE 24:27

And beginning with Moses and all the Prophets, he interpreted to them in all the Scriptures the things concerning himself.

QUESTION 7: According to these texts, what should we look for when we search the Scriptures? What do you think most people look for when they read the Bible? How does this relate to the main fight in the fight for joy that you studied in Lesson 5?

It is not only important that we search for the glory of Christ in Scripture, but that we seek the glory of Christ in prayer. Our prayers reveal the state of our hearts.

What a person prays for shows the spiritual condition of his heart. If we do not pray for spiritual things (like the glory of Christ, and the hallowing of God's name, and the salvation of sinners, and the holiness of our hearts, and the advance of the gospel, and contrition for sin, and the fullness of the Spirit, and the coming of the kingdom, and the joy of knowing Christ), then probably it is because we do not desire these things. Which is a devastating indictment of our hearts.

This is why J. I. Packer said, "I believe that prayer is the measure of the man, spiritually, in a way that nothing else is, so that how we pray is as important a question as we can ever face."[6]

QUESTION 8: Reflect on your most recent prayers. What do they reveal about the desires of your heart? If you are concerned about the nature of your prayers, what steps can you take to change them?

DAY 5: PREACHING AND THE FIGHT FOR JOY
Study the following passage.

PSALM 43

¹ Vindicate me, O God, and defend my cause against an ungodly people, from the deceitful and unjust man deliver me! ² For you are the God in whom I take refuge; why have you rejected me? Why do I go about mourning because of the oppression of the enemy? ³ Send out your light and your truth; let them lead me; let them bring me to your holy hill and to your dwelling! ⁴ Then I will go to the altar of God, to God my exceeding joy, and I will praise you with the lyre,

O God, my God. ⁵ *Why are you cast down, O my soul, and why are you in turmoil within me? Hope in God; for I shall again praise him, my salvation and my God.*

QUESTION 9: In this psalm, the psalmist is clearly distraught and cast down. Give three ways that the psalmist fights for joy in this passage.

As noted preacher and expositor Martyn Lloyd-Jones stated:

> Have you realized that most of your unhappiness in life is due to the fact that you are listening to yourself instead of talking to yourself? Take those thoughts that come to you the moment you wake up in the morning. You have not originated them but they are talking to you, they bring back problems of yesterday, etc. Somebody is talking. Who is talking to you? Your self is talking to you. Now this man's treatment [in Psalm 42] was this: instead of allowing this self to talk to him, he starts talking to himself. "Why art thou cast down, O my soul?" he asks. His soul had been depressing him, crushing him. So he stands up and says, "Self, listen for a moment, I will speak to you."[7]

Not only is it important that we preach to ourselves, it is vital that we regularly seek to hear the Word of God preached in the corporate gathering of believers.

Study 1 Corinthians 1:22-24 and 2 Timothy 3:16-4:2.

1 CORINTHIANS 1:22-24

22 For Jews demand signs and Greeks seek wisdom, 23 but we preach Christ crucified, a stumbling block to Jews and folly to Gentiles, 24 but to those who are called, both Jews and Greeks, Christ the power of God and the wisdom of God.

2 TIMOTHY 3:16-4:2

3:16 All Scripture is breathed out by God and profitable for teaching, for reproof, for correction, and for training in righteousness, 17 that the man of God may be competent, equipped for every good work. 4:1 I charge you in the presence of God and of Christ Jesus, who is to judge the living and the dead, and by his appearing and his kingdom: 2 preach the word; be ready in season and out of season; reprove, rebuke, and exhort, with complete patience and teaching.

QUESTION 10: According to these texts, what is the purpose of preaching in the life of the believer (i.e., the "called" of 1 Corinthians 1:22-24 and "the man of God" in 2 Timothy 3:16-4:2)? In your mind, why is it crucial for believers to regularly hear the Word of God preached?

This kind of speech has a spirit of exultation and seriousness about it. It is part of worship. When it is done in the power of the Holy Spirit, it *is* worship. It is expository exultation. The preacher worships over the Word that he proclaims. There is Spirit-given truth, and there is Spirit-given passion. And the effect on God's people is to awaken aspects of joy in Christ that may not come any other way. . . .

Studying the Word is good. Meditation is good. Discussion is good. Analyzing and explaining is good. But preaching is also good, and God calls us to enjoy the blessing that comes to us when the word of the cross explodes in the heart of a godly preacher and overflows in exultation to the minds and hearts of a worshiping people. The fight for joy loses one of its weapons when it does not regularly hear the gospel preached.[8]

FURTHER UP AND FURTHER IN

George Mueller (1805–1898) is famous for founding orphanages in Bristol, England, and depending upon God for all of his needs.

Read an article by John Piper entitled "A Taste of Mueller and His God" (www.desiringGod.org).

QUESTION 11: According to Mueller, what is the main point that we should seek to attain? How do we attain this goal?

Read the following quote from John Piper on the value of writing.

I have often counseled people who tell me that they don't see anything when they read the Bible, "Go home and this time, write the text, instead of just reading it. If anything stands out as helpful, make a mark and write down your ideas about it. Keep writing till you are done with that insight. Then keep reading and writing the text till you see something else, or until you are out of time." . . . Writing is a way of slowing us down and opening our eyes to see what we do not otherwise see. This struck me so forcefully one day that I paused and wrote:

I know not how the light is shed,
Nor understand this lens.
I only know that there are eyes
In pencils and in pens.[9]

QUESTION 12: What does John Piper mean by "there are eyes in pencils and in pens"? Why is writing such a helpful way to see things in the Bible?

Study Psalm 119:67 and Psalm 119:71.

PSALM 119:67

Before I was afflicted I went astray, but now I keep your word.

PSALM 119:71

It is good for me that I was afflicted, that I might learn your statutes.

QUESTION 13: According to these texts, what is the connection between suffering and Scripture? Why do you think this connection exists?

How often I am tempted to think that the pressures and conflict and frustrations are simply distractions from the business of ministry and Bible study. [Martin] Luther (along with Psalm 119:67, 71) teaches us to see it all another way. The stresses of life, the interruptions, the disappointments, the conflicts, the physical ailments, the losses—all of these may well be the very lens through which we see the meaning of God's Word as never before. Paradoxically, the pain of life may open us to the Word that becomes the pathway to joy.[10]

Read a sermon by John Piper entitled "Be Devoted to Prayer" (www.desiringGod.org).

QUESTION 14: According to John Piper, what are the three reasons *why* we should be devoted to prayer?

QUESTION 15: In this sermon, John Piper provides an acronym to help us become devoted to prayer. What is this acronym, and what does each letter stand for?

WHILE YOU WATCH THE DVD, TAKE NOTES

Record the first strategy that John Piper mentions as well as any sub-points of this strategy.

What is the second strategy that John Piper mentions?

List three characteristics or sayings of Jesus that cause John Piper to love Jesus.

1.

2.

3.

Why should we not skip the terrifying parts of the Bible?

What does I.O.U.S. stand for?

I

O

U

S

AFTER YOU WATCH THE DVD, DISCUSS WHAT YOU'VE LEARNED

1) Discuss the importance of Bible memorization in the fight for joy. What practical strategies are available to increase your Bible memorization?

2) Share one passage of Scripture that awakens a passion for Jesus in your soul.

3) Identify one or two factors that currently hinder your prayer life. What practical steps can you take to overcome these obstacles?

AFTER YOU DISCUSS, MAKE APPLICATION

1) What was the most meaningful part of this lesson for you? Was there a sentence, concept, or idea that really

struck you? Why? Record your thoughts in the space below.

2) Memorize the "I.O.U.S." verses (Psalm 119:36, Psalm 119:18, Psalm 86:11, and Psalm 90:14), and use them in your prayers before you read the Scriptures this week.

NOTES

1. Excerpt taken from *When I Don't Desire God*, pages 95-96.
2. Excerpt taken from *When I Don't Desire God*, page 102.
3. Excerpt taken from *When I Don't Desire God*, page 105.
4. Excerpt taken from *When I Don't Desire God*, page 125.
5. Excerpt taken from *When I Don't Desire God*, pages 148-149.
6. Excerpt taken from *When I Don't Desire God*, page 139.
7. Excerpt taken from *When I Don't Desire God*, page 81.
8. Excerpt taken from *When I Don't Desire God*, pages 77-79.
9. Excerpt taken from *When I Don't Desire God*, pages 123-124.
10. Excerpt taken from *When I Don't Desire God*, page 135.

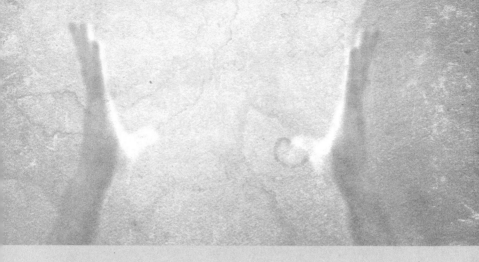

LESSON 7
STRATEGIES FOR THE FIGHT (PART 2)
*A Companion Study to the When I Don't Desire God DVD,
Session 6*

LESSON OBJECTIVES

It is our prayer that after you have finished this lesson . . .

> You will make a concerted effort to spend time with God-saturated people, both living and dead.

> You will be better equipped to use the natural world to fight for joy in God.

> You will be encouraged to fight for joy when the darkness doesn't lift.

BEFORE YOU WATCH THE DVD, STUDY AND PREPARE

DAY 1: THE COMMUNION OF SAINTS

Prayer and the Word of God are not the only weapons in the arsenal of the Christian. Fellowship with other believers is a crucial tool in the fight for joy.

Read 2 Corinthians 1:24, Hebrews 10:24-25, and Ephesians 4:29.

2 CORINTHIANS 1:24

Not that we lord it over your faith, but we work with you for your joy, for you stand firm in your faith.

HEBREWS 10:24-25

24 And let us consider how to stir up one another to love and good works, 25 not neglecting to meet together, as is the habit of some, but encouraging one another, and all the more as you see the Day drawing near.

EPHESIANS 4:29

Let no corrupting talk come out of your mouths, but only such as is good for building up, as fits the occasion, that it may give grace to those who hear.

QUESTION 1: According to these passages, what is the role of other Christians in the life of a believer? How can we fulfill this role for each other?

Examine Romans 1:9-12, 1 Thessalonians 3:9-10, and 2 John 12.

ROMANS 1:9-12

> [9] *For God is my witness, whom I serve with my spirit in the gospel of his Son, that without ceasing I mention you* [10] *always in my prayers, asking that somehow by God's will I may now at last succeed in coming to you.* [11] *For I long to see you, that I may impart to you some spiritual gift to strengthen you—* [12] *that is, that we may be mutually encouraged by each other's faith, both yours and mine.*

1 THESSALONIANS 3:9-10

> [9] *For what thanksgiving can we return to God for you, for all the joy that we feel for your sake before our God,* [10] *as we pray most earnestly night and day that we may see you face to face and supply what is lacking in your faith?*

2 JOHN 12

> *Though I have much to write to you, I would rather not use paper and ink. Instead I hope to come to you and talk face to face, so that our joy may be complete.*

QUESTION 2: Underline every phrase that refers to the result of a face-to-face meeting. Why do you think the apostles placed such an emphasis on meeting with believers face-to-face?

> All of us should feel the calling to exhort others with the Word of God. But that's not my point here. My point here is that you should make sure this is *done to you*. Put yourself

in some kind of fellowship, small enough so that this one-another ministry is happening. One of my first questions in dealing with a joyless saint is, "Are you in a small group of believers who care for each other and pray for each other and 'consider how to stir one another up to love'"?[1]

DAY 2: MEN OF WHOM THE WORLD WAS NOT WORTHY

It is not only living saints who encourage us. Godly saints who have come before us have the ability to speak to us, even though they are dead (Hebrews 11:4). John Piper testifies to the value of reading biographies of the saints.

For the sake of your joy in Christ read Christian biography. It will take you out of yourself and put you in another time and another skin, so that you see Jesus with eyes more full of wonder than your own. Find some Bible-saturated, God-centered saints from centuries gone by and learn from them how to fight for joy.[2]

QUESTION 3: Have you ever read the biography of a godly saint? Was your faith strengthened through the life of that saint? Record your reflections below.

In addition to reading biographies about godly saints, we should also avail ourselves of God-centered, Christ-exalting, intellectually rigorous, doctrinally rich works of theology. The modern tendency is to prefer the recent and light to the old and weighty. But C. S. Lewis shows us a more excellent way.

> For my own part, I tend to find the doctrinal books often more helpful in devotion than the devotional books, and I rather suspect that the same experience may await many others. I believe that many who find that "nothing happens" when they sit down, or kneel down, to a book of devotion, would find that the heart sings unbidden while they are working their way through a tough bit of theology with a pipe in their teeth and a pencil in their hand.[3]

QUESTION 4: How can doctrinal books produce passionate devotion? How would you respond to someone who thinks that hard thinking produces cold hearts?

DAY 3: CONNECTING THE NATURAL AND THE SPIRITUAL

The Bible endorses the use of the natural world in the fight for joy. After all, "the heavens declare the glory of God" (Psalm 19:1). But how exactly do we wield the world in the fight for joy?

Study the following passage.

1 TIMOTHY 4:1-5

> *1 Now the Spirit expressly says that in later times some will depart from the faith by devoting themselves to deceitful spirits and teachings of demons, 2 through the insincerity of liars whose consciences are seared, 3 who forbid marriage and require*

abstinence from foods that God created to be received with thanksgiving by those who believe and know the truth. [4] For everything created by God is good, and nothing is to be rejected if it is received with thanksgiving, [5] for it is made holy by the word of God and prayer.

QUESTION 5: According to this text, how should we receive gifts of God such as marriage and food? Think of at least three other natural things that can become means by which you pursue your joy in God. How can you use these things to worship God? Record your reflections below.

> The *direct* use of the physical world in our fight for joy may be a trip to the Grand Canyon, or rising early enough to see a sunrise, or attending a symphony, or reading a historical novel, or studying physics, or memorizing a poem, or swimming in the ocean, or eating a fresh pineapple, or smelling a gardenia blossom, or putting your hand through your wife's hair, or watching Olympic gymnastic finals. All these and a thousand things like them are *direct* ways of using the natural world to perceive more of the glory of God.[4]

As Christians we can use the world directly to perceive more of the glory of God, and we can use the world indirectly. For example, not only can we thank God for a hearty meal, but we also use the energy provided by the meal to strengthen us to do the work that God has called us to do.

QUESTION 6: Galatians 5:22 describes "patience" as a fruit of the Holy Spirit. However, many of us also discover that we tend to be more patient after we have received a good night's sleep. So which is it? Is patience the fruit of the Spirit or the fruit of sleep? Explain your answer.

DAY 4: PURSUING JOY IN GOD THROUGH SUFFERING

All human beings experience suffering in one form or another. Therefore, it is not strange that we would discuss suffering in a book about the fight for joy. Suffering can be one of the chief hindrances to lasting joy. But the Bible is shocking in the role it assigns to suffering in the Christian life.

Study the following passage.

ROMANS 5:3-5

> ³ *More than that, we rejoice in our sufferings, knowing that suffering produces endurance,* ⁴ *and endurance produces character, and character produces hope,* ⁵ *and hope does not put us to shame, because God's love has been poured into our hearts through the Holy Spirit who has been given to us.*

QUESTION 7: According to this text, how does suffering produce the joy of hope? How might this text be especially encouraging for someone who is unsure of his or her salvation?

This is God's universal purpose for all Christian suffering: more contentment in God and less satisfaction in self and the world. I have never heard anyone say, "The really deep lessons of life have come through times of ease and comfort." But I have heard strong saints say, "Every significant advance I have ever made in grasping the depths of God's love and growing deep with Him has come through suffering."[5]

Study the following passage.

ISAIAH 58:6-11

> [6] *Is not this the fast that I choose: to loose the bonds of wickedness, to undo the straps of the yoke, to let the oppressed go free, and to break every yoke?* [7] *Is it not to share your bread with the hungry and bring the homeless poor into your house; when you see the naked, to cover him, and not to hide yourself from your own flesh?* [8] *Then shall your light break forth like the dawn, and your healing shall spring up speedily; your righteousness shall go before you; the glory of the* LORD *shall be your rear guard.* [9] *Then you shall call, and the* LORD *will answer; you shall cry, and he will say, "Here I am." If you take away the yoke from your midst, the pointing of the finger, and speaking wickedness,* [10] *if you pour yourself out for the hungry and satisfy the desire of the afflicted, then shall your light rise in the darkness and your gloom be as the noonday.* [11] *And the* LORD *will guide you continually and satisfy your desire in scorched places and make your bones strong; and you shall be like a watered garden, like a spring of water, whose waters do not fail.*

QUESTION 8: How can we become springs of water that do not fail? Why is the promise in this verse counterintuitive?

God has made us to flourish by being spent for others. Jesus said, "It is more blessed to give than to receive" (Acts 20:35). Most of us do not *choose* against this life of outpouring; we *drift* away from it. We confuse pressured family life and stresses at work with Christian sacrifice, when in fact much of it has little to do with meeting the needs of the hungry and afflicted and perishing.

Please hear me carefully. This is not the diagnosis for all depression or discouragement. If it were, such self-giving servants would never be depressed. But they are. My point is that *one* of the causes of some people's darkness is a slowly creeping self-absorption and small-mindedness. And the cure may be the gradual embrace of a vision of life that is far greater than our present concerns.[6]

DAY 5: WHEN THE DARKNESS DOES NOT LIFT

Christian Hedonists are not naive. We are realists. We recognize that there are no quick fixes, no cure-alls, no miracle drugs. Walking the Calvary road with Christ is difficult. There may be seasons of doubt and depression and discouragement. This final section is meant to encourage you when the clouds of despair simply won't lift.[7]

Study the following passage.

PSALM 40:1-3

[1] *I waited patiently for the LORD; he inclined to me and heard my cry.* [2] *He drew me up from the pit of destruction, out of the miry bog, and set my feet upon a rock, making my steps secure.* [3] *He put a new song in my mouth, a song of praise to our God. Many will see and fear, and put their trust in the LORD.*

QUESTION 9: How does this psalm encourage us when we are in the pit of despair? Why is it significant that the psalmist does not tell us how long he waited?

> Saints who cry to the Lord for deliverance from pits of darkness must learn to wait patiently for the Lord. There is no statement about how long David waited. I have known saints who walked through eight years of debilitating depression and came out into glorious light. Only God knows how long we must wait. . . . We can draw no deadlines for God. He hastens or he delays as he sees fit. And his timing is all-loving toward his children. Oh, that we might learn to be patient in the hour of darkness. I don't mean that we make peace with darkness. We fight for joy. But we fight as those who are saved by grace and held by Christ.[8]

Study the following passage.

2 CORINTHIANS 1:3-9

> [3] Blessed be the God and Father of our Lord Jesus Christ, the Father of mercies and God of all comfort, [4] who comforts us in all our affliction, so that we may be able to comfort those who are in any affliction, with the comfort with which we ourselves are comforted by God. [5] For as we share abundantly in Christ's sufferings, so through Christ we share abundantly in comfort too. [6] If we are afflicted, it is for your comfort and salvation; and if we are comforted, it is for your comfort, which you experience when you patiently endure the same sufferings that we suffer. [7] Our hope for you is unshaken, for we know that as you share

in our sufferings, you will also share in our comfort. [8] *For we do not want you to be ignorant, brothers, of the affliction we experienced in Asia. For we were so utterly burdened beyond our strength that we despaired of life itself.* [9] *Indeed, we felt that we had received the sentence of death. But that was to make us rely not on ourselves but on God who raises the dead.*

QUESTION 10: Underline every phrase that refers to the purpose or result of affliction in this passage. In your own words, summarize this passage's teaching on the divine design in suffering. How can this help us when we are enduring the dark night of the soul?

FURTHER UP AND FURTHER IN

Study the following passage.

2 CORINTHIANS 8:1-4

[1] *We want you to know, brothers, about the grace of God that has been given among the churches of Macedonia,* [2] *for in a severe test of affliction, their abundance of joy and their extreme poverty have overflowed in a wealth of generosity on their part.* [3] *For they gave according to their means, as I can testify, and beyond their means, of their own accord,* [4] *begging us earnestly for the favor of taking part in the relief of the saints.*

QUESTION 11: According to this passage, where does abundant generosity come from? What is the most shocking thing about this passage to you?

Read Hebrews 11 in your own Bible.

QUESTION 12: Pick two of the saints from the "Hall of Faith," and meditate on the description of their lives in this passage. How do their lives strengthen your own faith? Record your reflections below.

For the past twenty years, John Piper has preached a biographical sketch of a prominent Christian at the annual Desiring God Conference for Pastors. These biographies are available for free at www.desiringGod.org.

Read (or listen to) one of the biographical sketches by John Piper (www.desiringGod.org).

QUESTION 13: How was your joy in Christ increased through learning about this saint? Record your reflections below.

QUESTION 14: One-third of our lives is spent sleeping. Presumably, there is a divine design in this reality. Speculate on the reasons why God ordained sleep. What does sleep teach us about ourselves and about God? If possible, cite Scripture in your answer.

Read a sermon by John Piper entitled "Sky Talk" (www. desiringGod.org).

QUESTION 15: At the end of this sermon, Piper lists eleven practical steps that his teacher Clyde Kilby used to stay alive to the beauty of God's world. Choose one of these steps and apply it to your own life. Record your reflections below.

WHILE YOU WATCH THE DVD, TAKE NOTES

What was the advice of John Piper's father when he was asked about how to fight for joy?

What is John Piper's eighth strategy in the fight for joy, and whom does he use to illustrate it?

What is the eleventh strategy that John Piper mentions?

What is Spurgeon's advice to those who spend most of their time indoors?

What mistake do many Christians make in the fight for joy (strategy 14)?

AFTER YOU WATCH THE DVD, DISCUSS WHAT YOU'VE LEARNED

1) Which of the strategies covered in this week's lesson was the most helpful to you? Why?

2) Discuss the various ways that other believers can be used by God in our fight for joy.

3) How does gaining a vision of God's global vision among unreached people groups aid us in the fight for joy?

AFTER YOU DISCUSS, MAKE APPLICATION

1) What was the most meaningful part of this lesson for you? Was there a sentence, concept, or idea that really struck you? Why? Record your thoughts in the space below.

2) Choose a part of this course that was meaningful to you, and seek to share it with another believer. Record your reflections on your conversation in the space below.

NOTES

1. Excerpt taken from *When I Don't Desire God*, page 130.
2. Excerpt taken from *When I Don't Desire God*, page 134.
3. Excerpt taken from *When I Don't Desire God*, page 127.
4. Excerpt taken from *When I Don't Desire God*, page 192.
5. Excerpt taken from *Desiring God*, page 265.
6. Excerpt taken from *When I Don't Desire God*, page 227.
7. For a short book-length treatment of this subject, see *When the Darkness Will Not Lift* by John Piper (Wheaton, IL: Crossway Books, 2006).
8. Excerpt taken from *When I Don't Desire God*, page 215.

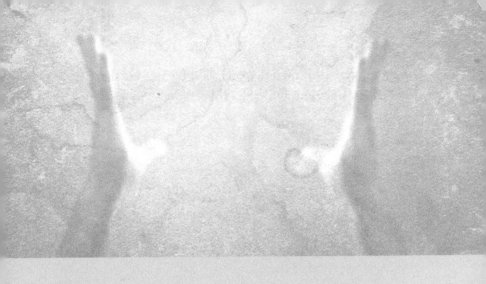

LESSON 8
REVIEW AND CONCLUSION

LESSON OBJECTIVES

It is our prayer that after you have finished this lesson . . .

> You will be able to summarize and synthesize what you've learned.

> You will hear what others in your group have learned.

> You will share with others how you have begun to see the gospel in a new light.

WHAT HAVE YOU LEARNED?

There are no study questions to answer in preparation for this lesson. Instead, spend your time writing a few paragraphs that explain what you've learned in this group study. To help you do this, you may choose to review the notes you've taken in the previous lessons. Then, after you've written down what you've learned, write down some questions that still remain in your mind about anything addressed in these lessons. Be prepared to share these reflections and questions with the group.

NOTES

Use this space to record anything in the group discussion that you want to remember.

LEADER'S GUIDE

AS THE LEADER OF THIS GROUP STUDY, *it is imperative that you are completely familiar with this study guide* and with the *When I Don't Desire God* DVD set. Therefore, it is our strong recommendation that you (1) read and understand the introduction, (2) skim each lesson, surveying its layout and content, and (3) read the entire Leader's Guide *before* you begin the group study and distribute the study guides. As you review this Leader's Guide, keep in mind that the material here is only a recommendation. As the leader of the study, feel free to adapt this study guide to your situation and context.

BEFORE LESSON 1

Before the first lesson, you will need to know approximately how many participants you will have in your group study. *Each participant will need his or her own study guide!* Therefore, be sure to order enough study guides. You will distribute these study guides at the beginning of the first lesson.

It is also our strong recommendation that you, as the leader, familiarize yourself with this study guide and the *When I Don't Desire God* DVD set in order to answer any questions that might arise and also to ensure that each group session runs smoothly and maximizes the learning of the participants. It is not necessary for you to preview *When I Don't Desire God* in its entirety—although it certainly wouldn't hurt!—but you should be prepared to navigate your way through each DVD menu.

NOTE: As we noted in the Introduction, this study guide is designed for an eight-session guided study. However, we understand that there are times when a group may only have six weeks with which to complete this study. In such a case, we recommend abbreviating Lesson 1 and completing it along with Lesson 2 in the first week. The preparatory work for Lesson 2 can be completed as a group during the first session. In addition, Lesson 8 may be completed by students on their own after the group has met for the final time.

DURING LESSON 1

Each lesson is designed for a one-hour group session. Lessons 2-8 require preparatory work from the participant before the group session. Lesson 1, however, requires no preparation on the part of the participant.

The following schedule is how we suggest that you use the first hour of your group study:

INTRODUCTION TO THE STUDY GUIDE (10 MINUTES)

Introduce this study guide and the *When I Don't Desire God* DVD. Share with the group why you chose to lead the group study using these resources. Inform your group of the commitment that this study will require and motivate them to work hard. Pray for the eight-week study, asking God for the grace you will need. Then distribute one study guide to each participant. You may read the introduction aloud, if you want, or you may immediately turn the group to Lesson 1 (starting on page 11 of this study guide).

PERSONAL INTRODUCTIONS (15 MINUTES)

Since group discussion will be an integral part of this guided study, it is crucial that each participant feels welcome and safe. The goal of each lesson is for every participant to contribute to the discussion in some way. Therefore, during these fifteen minutes, have the participants introduce themselves. You may choose to use the questions listed in the section entitled "About Yourself," or you may ask questions of your own choosing.

DISCUSSION (25 MINUTES)

Transition from the time of introductions to the discussion questions, listed under the heading "A Preview of *When I Don't Desire God*." Invite everyone in the class to respond to these questions, but don't let the discussion become too involved. These questions are designed to spark interest and generate questions. The aim is not to come to definitive answers yet.

REVIEW AND CLOSING (10 MINUTES)

End the group session by reviewing Lesson 1 with the group participants and informing them of the preparation that they must do before the group meets again. Encourage them to be faithful in preparing for the next lesson. Answer any questions that the group may have and then close in prayer.

BEFORE LESSONS 2-8

As the group leader, you should do all the preparation for each lesson that is required of the group participants—that is, the ten study questions. Furthermore, it is highly recommended that you complete the entire "Further Up and Further In" section. This is not required of the group participants, but it will enrich your preparation and will help you guide and shape the conversation more effectively.

The group leader should also preview the session of *When I Don't Desire God* that will be covered in the next lesson. So, for example, if the group participants are doing the preparatory work for Lesson 3, you should preview *When I Don't Desire God*, Session 2, before the group meets and views it. Previewing each session will better equip you to understand the material and answer questions. If you want to pause the DVD in the midst of the session in order to clarify or discuss, previewing the session will allow you to plan where you want to take your pauses.

Finally, you may want to supplement or modify the discussion questions or the application assignment. Please remember that *this study guide is a resource*; any additions or changes you make that better match the study to your particular group are encouraged. As the group leader, your own discernment, creativity, and guidance are invaluable, and you should adapt the material as you see fit.

Plan for about two hours of your own preparation before each lesson!

DURING LESSONS 2-7

Again, let us stress that during Lessons 2-7 you may use the group time in whatever way you desire. The following schedule, however, is what we suggest:

DISCUSSION (10 MINUTES)

Begin your time with prayer. The tone you set in your prayer will likely be impressed upon the group participants: if your prayer is serious and heartfelt, the group participants will be serious about prayer; if your prayer is hasty, sloppy, or a token gesture, the group participants will share this same attitude toward prayer. So model the kind of praying that you desire your students to imitate. Remember, the blood of Jesus has bought your access to the throne of grace.

After praying, review the preparatory work that the participants completed. How did they answer the questions? Which questions did they find to be the most interesting or the most confusing? What observations or insights can they share with the group? If you would like to review some tips for leading productive discussion, please turn to the appendix at the end of this book.

The group participants will be provided an opportunity to apply what they've learned in Lessons 2-7. As the group leader, you can choose whether it would be appropriate for the group to discuss these assignments during this ten-minute time-slot.

DVD VIEWING (30 MINUTES)[1]

Play the session for *When I Don't Desire God* that corresponds to the lesson you're studying. You may choose to pause the DVD at crucial points to check for understanding and provide clarification. Or you may choose to watch the DVD without interruption.

DISCUSSION AND CLOSING (20 MINUTES)

Foster discussion on what was taught during John Piper's session. You may do this by first reviewing the DVD notes (under the heading "While You Watch the DVD, Take Notes") and then proceeding to the discussion questions, listed under the heading "After You Watch the DVD, Discuss What You've Learned." These discussion questions are meant to be springboards that launch the group into further and deeper discussion. Don't feel constrained to cover these questions if the group discussion begins to move in other helpful directions.

Close the time by briefly reviewing the application section and the homework that is expected for the next lesson. Pray and dismiss.

BEFORE LESSON 8

It is important that you encourage the group participants to complete the preparatory work for Lesson 8. This assignment invites the participants to reflect on what they've learned and what remaining questions they still have. As the group leader, this would be a helpful assignment for you to complete as well. In addition, you may want to write down the key concepts of this DVD series that you want the group participants to walk away with.

DURING LESSON 8

The group participants are expected to complete a reflection exercise as part of their preparation for Lesson 8. The bulk of the group time during this last lesson should be focused on reviewing and synthesizing what was learned. Encourage all participants to share some of their recorded thoughts. Attempt to answer any remaining questions that they might have.

To close this last lesson, you might want to spend extended time in prayer. If appropriate, take prayer requests relating to what the participants have learned in these eight weeks, and bring these requests to God.

It would be completely appropriate for you, the group leader, to give a final charge or word of exhortation to end this group study. Speak from your heart and out of the overflow of joy that you have in God.

Please receive our blessing for all of you group leaders who choose to use this study guide:

> *The LORD bless you and keep you; the LORD make his face to shine upon you and be gracious to you; the LORD lift up his countenance upon you and give you peace. (Numbers 6:24-26)*

NOTES

1. Thirty minutes is only an approximation. Some of the sessions are shorter; some are longer. You may need to budget your group time differently, depending upon which session you are viewing.

APPENDIX
LEADING PRODUCTIVE DISCUSSIONS

Note: This material has been adapted from curricula produced by The Bethlehem Institute (TBI), a ministry of Bethlehem Baptist Church. It is used by permission.

IT IS OUR CONVICTION THAT the best group leaders foster an environment in their group that engages the participants. Most people learn by solving problems or by working through things that provoke curiosity or concern. Therefore, we discourage you from ever "lecturing" for the entire lesson. Although group leaders will constantly shape conversation, clarifying and correcting as needed, they will probably not talk for the majority of the lesson. This study guide is meant to facilitate an investigation into biblical truth—an investigation that is shared by the group leader and the participants. Therefore, we encourage you to adopt the posture of a "fellow-learner" who invites participation from everyone in the group.

It might surprise you how eager people can be to share what they have learned in preparing for each lesson. Therefore, you should invite participation by asking your group participants to share their discoveries. Here are some of our tips on facilitating discussion that is engaging and helpful:

> › Don't be uncomfortable with silence initially. Once the first participant shares his or her response, others will be likely to join in. But if you cut the silence short by prompting them, they are more likely to wait for you to prompt them every time.

> Affirm every answer, if possible, and draw out the participants by asking for clarification. Your aim is to make them feel comfortable sharing their ideas and learning; so be extremely hesitant to shut down a group member's contribution or trump it with your own. This does not mean, however, that you shouldn't correct false ideas— just do it in a spirit of gentleness and love.

> Don't allow a single person, or group of persons, to dominate the discussion. Involve everyone, if possible, and intentionally invite participation from those who are more reserved or hesitant.

> Labor to show the significance of their study. Emphasize the things that the participants could not have learned without doing the homework.

> Avoid talking too much. The group leader should not monopolize the discussion but rather guide and shape it. If the group leader does the majority of the talking, the participants will be less likely to interact and engage, and therefore they will not learn as much. Avoid constantly adding the "definitive last word."

> The group leader should feel the freedom to linger on a topic or question if the group demonstrates interest. The group leader should also pursue digressions that are helpful and relevant. There is a balance to this, however: the group leader *should* attempt to cover the material. So avoid the extreme of constantly wandering off topic, but also avoid the extreme of limiting the conversation in a way that squelches curiosity or learning.

> The group leader's passion, or lack of it, is infectious. Therefore, if you demonstrate little enthusiasm for the material, it is almost inevitable that your participants will likewise be bored. But if you have a genuine excitement for what you are studying, and if you truly think Bible study is worthwhile, then your group will be impacted

positively. Therefore, it is our recommendation that before you come to the group, you spend enough time working through the homework and praying so that you can overflow with genuine enthusiasm for the Bible and for God in your group. This point cannot be stressed enough. Delight yourself in God and in his Word!

⚹ desiringGod

If you would like to further explore the vision of God and life presented in this book, we at Desiring God would love to serve you. We have hundreds of resources to help you grow in your passion for Jesus Christ and help you spread that passion to others. At our website, desiringGod.org, you'll find almost everything John Piper has written and preached, including more than thirty books. We've made over twenty-five years of his sermons available free online for you to read, listen to, download, and in some cases watch.

In addition, you can access hundreds of articles, listen to our daily internet radio program, find out where John Piper is speaking, learn about our conferences, discover our God-centered children's curricula, and browse our online store. John Piper receives no royalties from the books he writes and no compensation from Desiring God. The funds are all reinvested into our gospel-spreading efforts. DG also has a whatever-you-can-afford policy, designed for individuals with limited discretionary funds. If you'd like more information about this policy, please contact us at the address or phone number below. We exist to help you treasure Jesus Christ and his gospel above all things because he is most glorified in you when you are most satisfied in him. Let us know how we can serve you!

Desiring God
Post Office Box 2901
Minneapolis, Minnesota 55402

888.346.4700
mail@desiringGod.org
www.desiringGod.org

Personal Notes

Personal Notes

Personal Notes

Personal Notes

Personal Notes

Personal Notes

Personal Notes

Personal Notes

Personal Notes